string

BARATARIA POETRY

Ava Leavell Haymon, Series Editor

ALSO BY MATTHEW THORBURN

Subject to Change
Disappears in the Rain
Every Possible Blue
This Time Tomorrow
A Green River in Spring
Dear Almost
The Grace of Distance

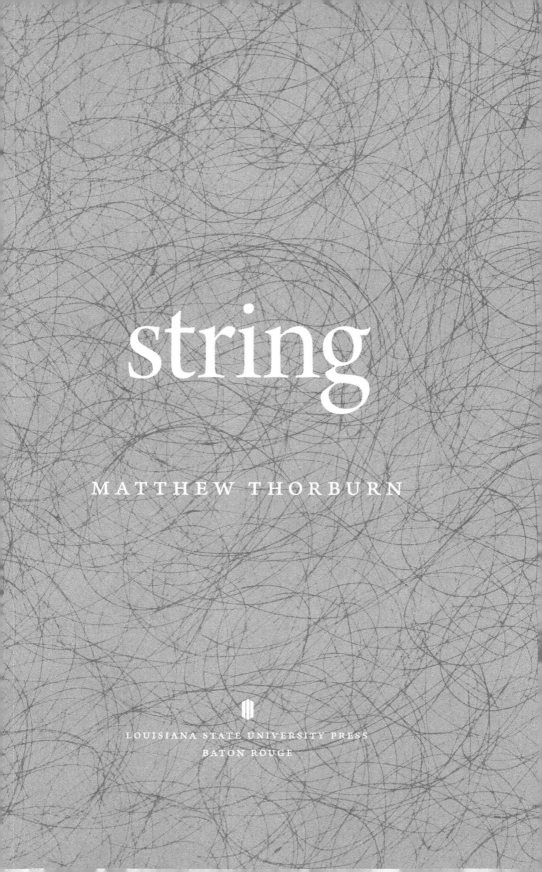

string

MATTHEW THORBURN

LOUISIANA STATE UNIVERSITY PRESS

BATON ROUGE

Published by Louisiana State University Press
lsupress.org

LSU Press Paperback Original

DESIGNER: Michelle A. Neustrom
TYPEFACE: Arno Pro

Cover illustration courtesy iStock.com/Tevarak.

LIBRARY OF CONGRESS CATALOGING-IN-PUBLICATION DATA
Names: Thorburn, Matthew, author.
Title: String / Matthew Thorburn.
Description: Baton Rouge : Louisiana State University Press, [2023] |
   Series: Barataria poetry
Identifiers: LCCN 2022042810 (print) | LCCN 2022042811 (ebook) | ISBN
   978-0-8071-7904-8 (paperback) | ISBN 978-0-8071-7989-5 (pdf) | ISBN
   978-0-8071-7988-8 (epub)
Subjects: LCGFT: Poetry.
Classification: LCC PS3620.H76 S77 2023 (print) | LCC PS3620.H76 (ebook) |
   DDC 811/.6—dc23/eng/20220909
LC record available at https://lccn.loc.gov/2022042810
LC ebook record available at https://lccn.loc.gov/2022042811

let all things go free that have survived

—SEAMUS HEANEY

contents

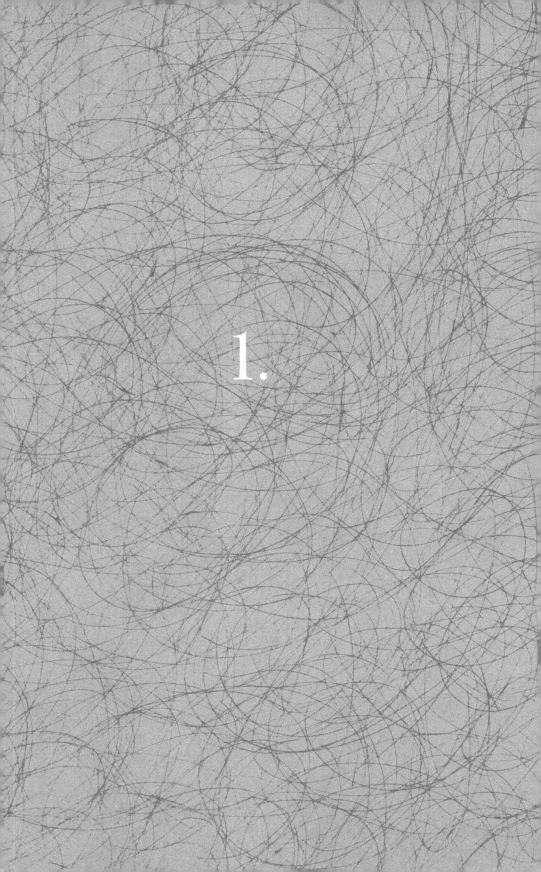

1.

Once

there was crusty bread
a last half-loaf a rind of cheese
my parents danced in

the empty kitchen they knew
we would never come back
they didn't know

I listened in the dark
brush and scuff of shoes
guttering candle

there was no moon there was
a broken oak a silvery rain
pooling in the grass

once in the tall grass there
was a tan captain
chest smooth pants unbuttoned

his holster amazed him
by being empty
Rosie groaned spat clutched

her wrinkled pink dress
pointed the pistol
between his eyes between

the trees I saw how
everyone dies but once I was
a boy who talked in circles

talked in circles I walked
in the woods there was
nowhere I wouldn't follow her.

The Musicians

after Pablo Picasso's *Three Musicians,* oil on canvas, 1921

Uncle Albert laughed he sat backwards on the piano stool he reached back
for a chord a halting melody

Roger slipped in under the piano he barked once twice his tail keeping time
between Jean's feet

Jean with his scratched glasses Father's oldest friend Jean with his limp that
didn't matter now his clarinet's starry-night shine its husky groan

before one song could end another began first "Weary Blues" then "Dead
Man Blues" then "Stoptime Rag"

piano hands Mother called it how Uncle Albert's moved even on the couch
even drifting off fingers shaping chords in his sleep

Father tapped the piano lid like a drum Aunt Adelaide strummed her
washboard with thimbled fingers Mother sang "Honeysuckle Rose"

the best songs are fast songs Uncle Albert said they end too soon

streetlamp light slipped between the blinds it fell in stripes over their
shoulders over mine

because I played too my violin light as a bird under the bow I was afraid to let
go so sure it would fly.

Pipistrello

Father called you in the old
tongue used only with Mother
which suits your jaunty
dart and stitch your glide
and swoop much better than

our flat no-nonsense *bat*
you sew up the night
out and over trees the pond
the field you gather loose ends
you loop around again

zip and stir swerve strike
pluck bugs from air
you fly by ear I remember
the teacher taught us
(I remember the teacher

one night hanged upside down
in a tree) can I say you see
with your ears are mostly
fuzzed wings then vanish
as I would've except

I had none and nowhere
to go now it's dusk
and you one shade lighter
than dusk o bobbin
o fillip of fear flying up

away like the tailor's needle
a silver sweep and flash
you at home here in the dark
where we groped we worried
we wished for light.

My Picture of Father

Someone snapped him
about to marry my mother
my I say though they
had yet to imagine me

but always I will see him
slouching in the kitchen after
Uncle Albert dragged him out
all night laughing so much

singing a taste of beer
still in his mouth and now
how early how sunny
the window a square of white

blanking out Schmidt's farm
his dark hair shiny
his tie not tied no way
he could know what awaits

which makes me love him
even more makes me
worry though it's too soon
too late let me show you how

time stops the camera
says let me show you
how time hurtles on leaves
only this creased piece

of cardboard little square
I carry in my pocket how
brave he looks or how scared
if there's a difference.

My Picture of Mother

There is no matching
photograph of Mother
almost still a girl and so
skinny her fair hair

braided too busy
climbing into
her complicated white
dress upstairs

in her own mother's
house why so
many hooks and eyes
she thinks why

can you not sit still
her mother wonders
aloud cinching
her in knowing her

daughter will
never get to sit still
what Mother hoped
for wished or

worried over
I'll never know
I was too young to
know how to ask.

A Little

the tailor said letting out
Rosie's pale yellow dress so
it hung right then a little
later taking it in again

so it hung right he made
the sewing machine go
his foot upon the treadle
how it hummed his hands

free to hold the worn cloth
a little to the right or left
no time for more than a little
as the carnival moved on

the soldiers moved in darkness
fell down and they're gone
Mother's silly words before sleep
Father's spectacles folded

away in his pocket how
Uncle Albert held his stick
just so the way this story ends
I can't remember except

so soon too soon be sure
to leave it a little better than
you found it Mother taught
but she did say leave it.

Her Breath

We sat once in a field of summer grass and buttercups

one after another after another

Rosie leaned back on her elbows in her yellow dress

her tan legs stretched out before her

her brown dog Roger stretched out beside her

what a perfect word

buttercup I just wanted to say buttercup I would've

kept saying buttercup buttercup but

for heaven's sake she breathed against my ear

stop talking about flowers.

Saltzman

slouched in his doctor's coat   not white anymore and frayed

at the cuffs always   with tea steeping a few loose

cigarettes on his desk   late one night he came to see

Mother finally it was   time for Little Brother to come

but he never arrived he   missed his train Father said

squeezing my shoulder not   looking at me dear

Doctor Saltzman your pocket watch   ticked like a bomb

your head a speckled egg   the soldiers laughed and cracked open.

They

liked to throw things
a man down a well a woman
through a window they

liked to know things
names and dates your hopes
what hurt my hiding place

the combination to Saltzman's
empty safe they liked to
break things doors bicycles

legs and backs and necks
they liked to take things
money gold rings fingernails

and fathers they had
no need for her none for me
except they were hungry so

hungry and so angry
like shadows they liked to hide
behind my back they liked

to ride behind my eyelids
death was their dark horse
they never stood still.

A Damaged Animal

The poor white upright
piano scored with
bullet holes they shot it too

then tipped it off
the balcony mangling Rosie's

silver bicycle forever
after a damaged animal
the white keys broken

teeth in the gutter
where their piss trickled

the black keys like
fingers broken in
black gloves.

Respair

Jean whispered in
my ear but only later
I learned it meant *gain hope*
the opposite of *despair*
which felt impossible

even if he was French
clean shaven and still
played his *licorice*
stick Mother called it
now they will never

come back he said
listening to the silence
that used to be starlings
jays mourning doves
even sparrows that was

the last time I saw Mother
cry I do not want to see
any more Jean said
he took off his spectacles
and laughed how long

since I heard a laugh
he did it just once as if
he changed his mind
he stood by the bare tree
broken in two as if

lightning had struck
and not a bomb he said
those wishing to sing
will always find a song
but he only spoke.

The River's Song

I would sing you

a sky of finger-smudged glass
spikes of wild asparagus

in the wet ditch beside the road

Rosie roll out the piano please
the old white upright in need of a tune-up

the yellow elbow of the river

in what's left of the light
the river that remembers and forgets

a bright blade

of light glances off the trees
the trees glance back

a bright blade

the river that forgets and remembers
in what's left of the light

the yellow elbow of the river

the old white upright in need of a tune-up
Rosie won't you please roll out the piano

beside the wet ditch beside the road

spikes of wild asparagus
a sky of finger-smudged glass

I will sing you.

A Bath

after Pierre Bonnard's *Nude in Bathtub*,
oil on canvas, c. 1940–1946

I remember its milky curvy bulk
perched on dainty claw feet
watery blue bathroom tiles
the rush and crash
of water from the taps I remember

the long brown whip of him
Roger stretched across the green
and yellow rug the damp air
steamed-up mirror she looked
over her white shoulder she
looked again I remember her

pruney fingertips tapping the tooth-
colored tub the chipped
and yellowing tub the squeal
of the old metal taps I don't
remember how we got there only
how slowly Rosie finger-combed
the dark hair behind my ears.

The Magician

The white rabbit popping out of a hat I loved best so plump its sleepy stillness

and the bright rings that were linked then not then clinked together again

like Rosie's hand like mine held tight then let go the colored scarves

red after blue after green a wave a rope like magic

the way they made me forget

the bomb-splintered tree out back its branches scattered in a halo

there was time for one last trick

the turban'd magician his skinny assistant in her sparkly mask

smile a finger snap and poof

they made themselves vanish him and her both at once

no one left to say ta-da

I squeezed Rosie's hand heard her mother cough

in that darkness I thought of Grandfather deaf in one ear

his left hand Mother would say just didn't work anymore too tired

I thought of his heavy walking stick the newspaper folded on his chair

how it did not disappear for a year it was the day he died.

The Boot

From the cracked attic
window we counted
ragged soldiers stumbling

across Schmidt's field
coatless muddy one

bloodied a broken rifle
for a crutch Aunt Adelaide
squinted through

Father's black binoculars
whose side are they on

she wondered I wished
they would get away
go away but a bald man

on horseback crashed
out of the sycamores
sword flashing white

a colonel maybe a major
we shouted down

to Mother but oh
Adelaide cried dear lord
another horse broke

from the burnt trees
circling red-flanked

no rider only still
stuck in one stirrup
an empty boot.

Pale Stars

I saw Rosie suddenly after
looking a long time
into purple irises untouched
beside the burnt wreck

the blackened plane took off
half her house my knees
ached from crouching low
last ribbons of smoke

acrid stink in my throat
days I dreamed green
fingers in the dirt no one
said stop growing no

one said hold your breath
but then I saw her
hair her dress just darker
than irises a bare

shoulder she hunched
purple in the purple-gray
caught the same fading
light in worried folds

at first I could not
see her could've stared
hand to brow hand
to brow and never seen

but then the bells
of her sleeves her hands
white stars cut out
everything else was dirt

was broken buried
I looked longer lower long
pale thighs a smear
of blood a handprint

bruised dark she
crouched in flowers
a spreading
shadow on the torn-up

ground I couldn't
stop looking she
turned she saw me
run Rosie mouthed run.

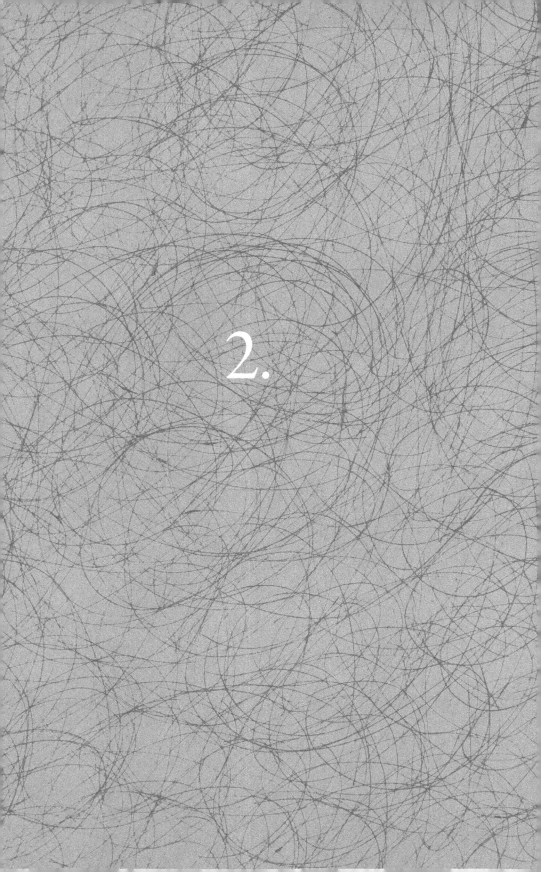

2.

Which Way Now

I thought I saw you stepping
into the street heard you
tapping at the window
whispering my name once
you pinched my elbow

in the tall grass your hair
hanging over my face almost
kissing me then kissing me
there when I wanted you
which was always which was

sitting on a speckled rock
by the cold river your hands
hiding scraped knees
walking the muddy road
you gulped from my canteen

a thread of water
silvering your long neck
once in Schmidt's field
we crouched between rows
of green your finger to my lips

a soldier ran past I stared
at the dirt on your toes
tasted dirt on your finger once
you slipped into the shadow
between two trees once

the amber light falling in
the river so I looked
in its broken mirrors its
galloping horses I wandered
the woods calling Rosie

Rosie in the fields the barn
I waited I wondered when
would you be back
I searched the shuttered
post office torn letters

under my feet under
the stars I called until
I heard thought I heard
you asking where
could we ever be safe?

Stories We Do Not Tell

The firing squad stood waiting

in a cold drizzle he'd made

his last request but no one thought

bring an umbrella no one

thought poor man yesterday still mayor

today can't get his cigarette lit

too soggy too windy Old Schmidt

leaned on his hoe watching it

not happen watching rain bounce

off the gray river his tired brown cow

my heart like a house I thought

crouching in a doorway's shadow

like four small rooms swept clean

closing my eyes I heard birds

chattering thieving fallen

grain from the field then gunshots

then silence then birds chattering again

I know better now my heart's not

a house only a heart running down

here's the fast dark water

once I walked into a heavy stone

in each pocket but changed

my mind let them go by the time

I got home my clothes were dry.

To Tighten and to Tune

A noun like a nail
Father called
out a verb
the quick hammer

to pound it
home he said
because he made
words stand

still mean what
they were
meant to mean
because speaking

softly at the sink
he washed
grease
from the creases

of his hands
said all questions
must end
in the curious

vise-grip
of a question mark
or should they
would they because

he waited
while I leaned closer
in the kitchen's
dim light

to read
the words laid out
like ratchets
wrenches washers

because he
guided me through
each sentence
until its wheels

turned liquid-
smooth
make words
do their work

he said checking
the bolts
of periods commas
ear cocked

for the scrape
and whine
of a slipping gear
because now

I take up
his pen to tighten
to tune
sentences re-

worked until
they break
the hurt they
make a song.

Shatterings

Thin silvery fish carried home from the river   six or seven on a brown string

dashes of bright yellow chalk   the tailor marked my sleeves my cuffs

Mother changed each day like the weather   sun thunder gathering clouds

papers burning in the fireplace   Father fed them into the fire

the doorframe splintered a soldier kicked down the door

✺

gray helmets rising past our feet   muddy boots thumping up the stairs

drawers yanked emptied out   glass-glitter on the window sill

a book flapped down   torn pink nightgown snagged in a tree

there was nothing there   was nothing left alone

a scream someone screaming I realized it was me

⁂

Mother's brown shoe   brimmed with rain

the back wall rubbled bricks   a soldier smoked and laughed

empty cigarette case cracked white vase   Grandmother's portrait kicked in

the scratched black piano   hunched over its broken leg

but still Tuesday still morning but no birds sang

※

a handful of blackberries   in a chipped blue bowl

we could leave tonight or tomorrow   Father said right now or never

a gleaming spoon   last dollop of sweet cream

there was no time   there was nothing but time

light fell through the leaves like broken glass.

After His Stroke

Uncle Albert frowned
he slouched once
more at the piano
one hand on the keys

the four keys he kept
touching tapping he
kept pressing
sometimes pounding

afternoons a faint
tickle a stutter of
knots nots notes nights
and days he kept at it

jumbled letters a ring
of jangling keys
that tangle of strings
he kept looking for

the combination to
melody to set off
a song take him
back to "Maple Leaf

Rag" or "The Easy
Winners" the tune his
lips couldn't make shapes
to say the song his

foot once kept time to
his fingers could play
all night especially when
he closed his eyes.

After the Bomb

Bits of paper swirled behind my eyes

some with treble clefs with quarter

or half notes Uncle Albert penciled

years ago no longer a waltz a serenade

but the hum that follows fell

over his charred blue armchair

one arm blown off the chandelier

a spray of powdery glass

burnt carpet turning white under

paper flakes fake snow the night's

first faint stars twinkling overhead

because no ceiling now no roof.

Wouldn't Hold

Everything is made of
loops made of long
lines Mother said and it
began to unravel

the string of the world
running out of my pencil
she taught me to hold on
fingers' pressure

against wood could blur
lead to shadow show
the slow darkening
a candle's flicker making

strange angles of her face
she said it all fades
is lost to the horizon
she snuffed the flame and

I was falling I tried to
slide inside my letters
p's open window
the low doorway of an *h*

but how could I know
words wouldn't hold me
how could I know
they close so tight.

The Barn

Old Schmidt clacked
two sticks to tell
his sheep it's time for bed
he smelled like a barn

Mother said gray overalls
always muddy always
something filthy
in his hands a hoe or rake

a snake a dead bird
a wiry dog trotted alongside
dirty as he was
tin bell around its neck

so weird familiar music
comes drifting back
bark jingle mutter clack
and fades away

they were a little family
it's true it's time
he called time to go back
over the hill into the barn

where he did sometimes
drowse beside them
where he was happiest
there in the dry hay

the sagging gray barn
they locked up they
burned down one night
all the sheep inside.

Get Away Get Away

after Pablo Picasso's *Man with a Lamb,* cast bronze sculpture, 1943

I pulled her in my arms   lifted her bulk heavier

than I thought gawky and   awkward so hot she was

shaking bleating I couldn't   see I wanted to save

something burning the barn   burning smoke in my mouth

searing and I couldn't find   anyone who was there

I couldn't know except there   the orange flames jumped

across her eyes they hurt   my lungs her flanks

wet where skin had been   she pissed no air she shat

no breath all she wanted   was beyond the bright was

get away get away   was run back into the fire.

Once Our Garden

What did the brown dog
know we didn't
his nose down eager panting
ribs like an accordion his
scrabbling claws unearthed
white thin crooked
fingers Father yanked
him back Mother pushed me
away don't look don't look
but I saw the hound's
wide yellow eye his claws
Father's raw hands scraping
away at what was once
our garden what was
pale silk pink lipstick mouth
full of dirt black hair
stuck to her face her face
she was seventeen still
dressed for a party
Rosie's brown eyes open
I tried to lift her
head turned all the way
around like an owl.

Couldn't Let Go

How could we stay   or go or   wait and go later could we

run jump a train pray   for fog to drift   over us instead of

bombs the bridge stopped now   halfway across the river as if

it changed its mind   the church gone Schmidt's barn gone

rocks in the well salt in the fields   and Rosie   a cat picked at

something bloody in a puddle   Mother buttoned my coat

she said David she looked   at me she said David

that was Father's name too   she gripped his arm there was

something she needed   to go back for what

couldn't she let go   she didn't say   I'll never know

I'll meet you   there she said   we'll take the train she said

he said Angela please   kiss me she said don't   say goodbye.

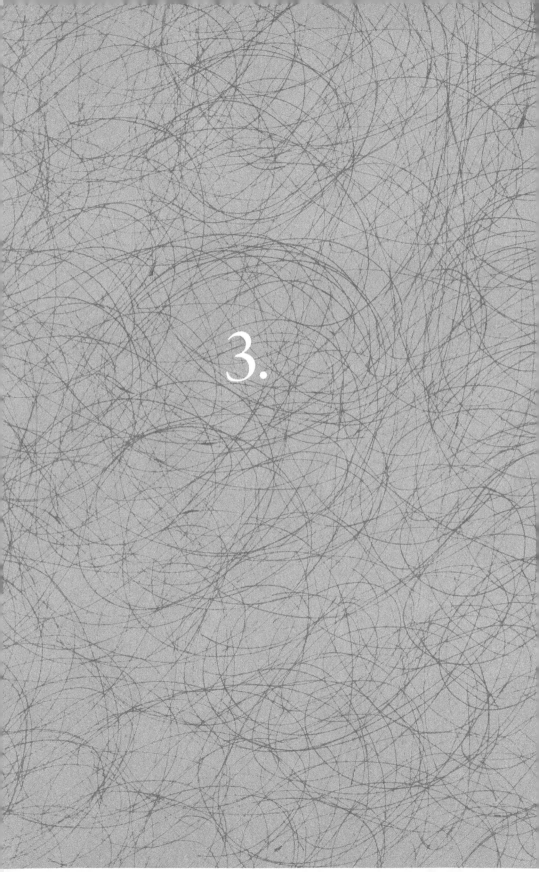

3.

There's This String

I follow I don't
know what
else I can do
sometimes
yanking it hand
over hand
sometimes just
inching along
looping it
up lassoing
it around
my left elbow
I ease it
out a centi-
meter or
millimeter
at a time
each knot
I tease loose I
tie and re-
tie pull
myself up by
I climbed out
of the well
when the only
sound left
was water
dripping
the wind
pushed me
along drops
running
down
this long string

I slipped from
the attic after
the boots
drifted away
crunching
bits of glass
angry
talk fading
to a hum
this string
taut still
damp chafing
my hands
I followed it
down the dark
fold-away
attic steps
something
inside me is
raveling
unraveling
something's
disappearing
into deep
starless night
I followed it
between
rows of tanks
between
green tentfuls
of soldiers
sleeping
this string
stretching

through drifts
of pale smoke
Mother
where are
you Father
where are you
hold on
he said
please don't
let go
I said
one end
looped
around my
wrist
knotted tight
one end
circling his
the train
station jammed
so crowded
this is how
we'll keep
together
Father said
every-
one was
leaving or
trying to leave
everyone was
running or
trying to
run through
the crush of

bodies bodies
steam smoke ash
falling
like snow
so many
brown suitcases
held shut
with string
pants cinched
up with string
bundles
of account
books a red
wool blanket
photographs in
scratched
wooden frames
maps family
trees carpets
rolled up
tied tight
with string
and no trains
arriving
no trains
leaving
hold on
Father said
you'll find me
here at the
other end
he said
so I did
I do

I clench
my fists I pull
myself along
careful so care-
ful not to
let it go
let it break
I keep
inching
forward I slip
handfuls
fistfuls
into my pocket
sometimes
a shoelace
twisty gray
twine broken
knotted
back together
sometimes
a rope I
swing from
my last
violin string
a frayed
strand of yarn
from Aunt
Adelaide's bright
blue scarf
the bit of white
cooking string
Mother tied
around her
ring finger

to remind her
of what
a fine filament
of Minsky's yellow
thread un-
spooling flying
free of
the clattering
sewing machine
heavy as
an anchor
a piano
wire that hums
"Heliotrope
Bouquet" all
the way back
to the long
white key
beneath Uncle
Albert's finger
it might be
the gray
telephone
line a springy
coil the soldiers'
razor wire
a loosened
belt a lightning bolt
Rosie's
dark shining
ponytail
I always wanted
to touch
and never got

to touch
enough
silky braid
heavy as
a bell-pull
hanging
to her waist
it swung when
she walked
I would have
followed her
anywhere
as long as she
let me
this string is
the fuse
I won't light
keep the kitchen
match away
the umbilical
cord Little
Brother
it wouldn't let
you go
let you breathe
it's the line
I've drawn
the one I hold
tight
that holds us
together
like cursive
lacing one
letter to the next

this tangle
of words
I keep
saying out
loud repeating
repeating
so it won't end so
I can reach
its other end
where you
will all be
waiting
or never get
there
never know
you're
not coming back
sometimes
I want
to cut it
be quiet be
done lie
down in the dark
but I don't
have scissors
Mother's
rusty pair
I dropped
in the ditch
I won't
break it
with my teeth
I'll leave this
last knot

unpicked
won't let go
watch it
spring back
into shadow
this string
I follow
as the days
drag by
the nights
wander on
as I grow
tired grow
older
this string
puddles
around my feet
trips
me up
slows
me down
a river rushing
away
behind me
river that
remembers and
forgets
and remembers
my words
floating away
this
pile of string
a trail in
the snow

a track in
the ash
like a sign like
a clue a story a
song oh
where does it
come from
oh where
am I going
this string
I follow
and follow and
know I can
never stop.

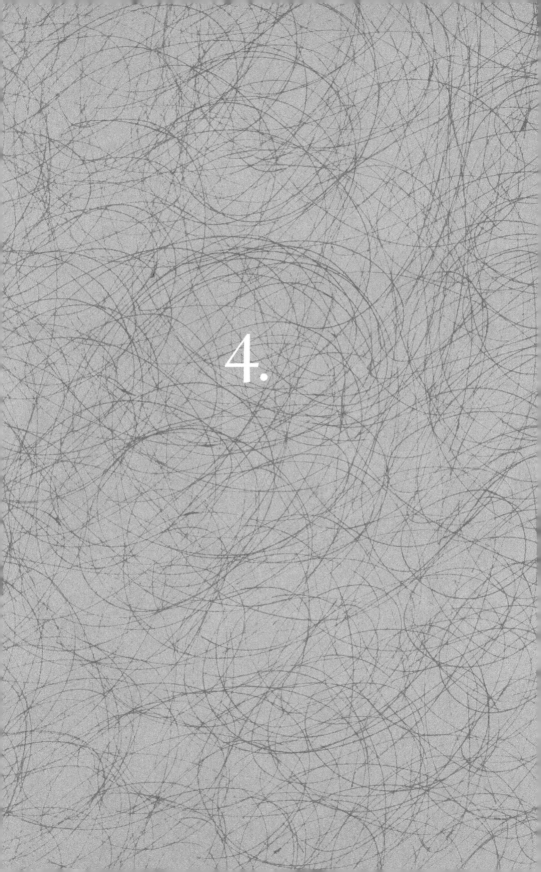

4.

Mother's Silver Teapot

we buried in the garden
before we left for
safe keeping Father said
until we are thirsty

again Mother laughed
and looked away
so long after the fighting
was over I went back

a whole day digging
in places I thought
I remembered and
never found it

though our brass 27
still hung there beside
no door and past
the doorframe no house.

Each Night We Wandered

Father's boots came from two
different bodies his jacket
had bullet holes in the back
another over his heart

still warm he whispered
poking a finger through
I closed my eyes and it was
dark I opened my eyes

and it was dark this went on
and on and somewhere
somehow someone
was playing the piano

I thought now I'm dreaming
but Father heard too
just black keys he said
what else was left the radio

lost in our leaving
but still we heard static
smoke worry clouds of ash
but still the moon rose

each night I wandered
sleeping a little in the fields
a catnap Father said a rabbit's
rest but not the wet ditch

not the muddy furrows
where Old Schmidt
the farmer lay stretched
in the dirt eyes open mouth

bloody bible pages scattered
keep sleeping he whispered
did I say the radio was gone
Father kept it turned low

I tried to guess where
I wandered by the songs
the rain's strange music
kept playing all night.

Doctor Saltzman's Black Bag

sat stiffly on our table
mouth open wide
a stethoscope I remember
curled inside its silver
fish eye bright always

cold against my chest
I am very sorry
he kept his gray hands
busy tidying I didn't
realize who he was

speaking to but
there was only me
I remember I felt far
away felt like someone
else I wished I was

my brother lost
before he'd arrived
how early he said
the trees have turned
he closed his case

I closed my eyes
listening hard as if
I might hear each
blood-red leaf
break upon our roof.

The Fisherman

What was he hauling up
from the cold river
grizzled fisherman
going at it hand
over hand at the end

of the dock the coarse
rope coiled behind him
the other darker end
wetting his chapped hands
frayed pants he fought

against the weight of it
a heavy silver fish
I hoped but couldn't
understand what I saw
when it broke the surface

swinging up tumbling
onto the dock he dropped
the rope hurried to scoop
them up toss them
in his dented gray bucket

before they slipped away
black eels wriggling
where the jaw had been
the eyes in the rotting
horse head he used for bait.

Disappear

Once I thought I could step

off the bank drift away

only a faint blue string

to hold onto something

scrawled in chalk

beside the broken piano

too hard to make out

rain blurred the wind

carried off unless you stood

close in the dark closed

your eyes who would miss

a fifteen-year-old boy

dirty and tired hungry

a name not worth calling

after all Mother

disappeared in the dark

Aunt Adelaide ran

into a bullet Uncle Albert fell

asleep in a snowstorm

of white pills I saw how

it wouldn't be hard

the only way if you could

go nowhere else

and when I said *you* I knew

I meant me because

already you were gone

Father fallen into

the wet ditch by the road

too many holes in your back

to float I saw how

I could step into the river so

fast so cold I could put

a heavy stone in each pocket

and keep walking.

Where She Went

Mother tunneled   under the fence maybe caught the last

bus the last train she   flew away like the last

lark I haven't seen one   for weeks one foot in front

of the other she'd say so   maybe she walked away

climbed a hill crossed   the mountains

she drifted away   the way a song does into your ear

into the air she   slipped under Grandfather's black hat

left her reflection   in the glow of Jean's clarinet

she swirled with the last   hot water down the drain

maybe into the breath   between "Bucket's Got a Hole"

and "Keyhole Blues"   she cut the light

unzipped her   shadow I wanted to

hold on but Father   let go of her hand so she

wouldn't disappear   the way he did wouldn't reappear

the way he did   face in the mud.

What's Left to Tell

I remember icy water hauled up
in a bucket from a well

after I found him again before
I lost him again

and the wooden chest he tore apart
with a claw hammer for a fire

my name is not Jean
said Jean my hands are not
my hands are not done shaking

I remember the scar I could see
when he faced the light

so hungry once he tried to eat
his shoelaces he sighed the buttons
right off his shirt he muttered

and then because it was green
he said even his shirt

well first just the collar
but then the cuffs and then

he knew where we were by looking at
the stars he knew how
to make me believe he did

on his arm a tattoo of a knife
in his hand a knife

one Sunday they found us

they cut down the church bell
it clanged against the ground

they hanged him with the rope

no I won't tell won't tell it that way
that way it was only

a gray bucket I remember
banging the bottom of a well.

The Stag

after Gerhard Richter's *Stag (Hirsch)*,
oil on canvas, 1963

I couldn't see a way out
for him the woods
too tangled those arrowing
branches pinned him in
one broad trunk weighed

him down no break
in sight no light shafting
through and what did you do
I lay still among the bodies
and how did you live

I played dead as the dead
grew cold all night
and why didn't you scream
I did scream down
in the dark I kept it locked

behind my teeth and why
did you close your eyes
so I could see the stag instead
his head turned to me
I watched until he blurred

away into pale gray light
and why tell us this
because I've grown old because
my punishment for living
is to keep living.

Let Her

read a letter the one   I never wrote I couldn't send

let her catch   her breath

know I wish   I wrote Rosie wrote   love me leave with me

let her climb   a ladder leap into

a train instead of

the dusk the down the dirt

how I wish her   this blank page this snowed-in field

untouched by   any hand or foot for

filling in or not   a letter or not let her   write a song and

sing herself into it draw   a picture and slip into that

landscape let her   leave this   behind let her run

away   be angry and loud alone but alive

let her pull the trigger again and again and

on top of her   nothing   but the terrible stars.

I Remember He Was Like a Dancer

The bald tailor with a limp
piece of black thread
hanging from his mouth

like a damp whisker
how he bent to his work
even if his hands ached

the long needle would glint
a sliver of light between
finger and thumb he took

up the heavy wool
each cuff held in place
a few pins slipped in

the gray pins he re-used
the forty spools of thread
every shade he knew

he could find one it would
blend in make him
an invisible line that held

wait Rosie said I want you
to see something
beautiful she kissed me

pulled me down to
peek in a low window
after dark he slipped

the soft blue the flowery
silk dress I'd never
see Mother wear again

over his bare shoulders
under the lone bulb
he danced a last waltz.

Until You Never

Backwards I would tell it
so the soldiers borrow the rope
from Jean's neck to hang
the church bell so rocks fly
from windows and sparkly bits
rise into frames so flames
turn into Schmidt's barn

a crackling torch a glass bottle
drop into a soldier's hands
I would tell it backwards
so the bleating sheep go quiet
the lightning-cracked sky
lightens in the west the sheep

wander backwards out
of the barn soldiers climb back
into their trucks their tanks
roll slowly out of sight rifles
suck up each bullet as they go

so Mother will appear here
beside me again I'll drift
awake again she strokes my hair
her warm hand my sweet boy

a dream she says a dream
you must wake up now it's time
to turn on the light time to

get dressed eat dinner grow
smaller until you never have to

live through this.

A Girl Was Singing

Once a dog ran into the road
and a girl hurried after him calling
Roger Roger as the mechanic

struck a match on his boot sole
the butcher wiped his hands
on his apron stained pink

once in the field outside town
birds chattered and then
a gun cracked then silence

then the birds chattering again
faint but once a little string of notes
even this shy boy heard it

he let the sheet music drift
to the floor set down his violin
leaned out the window

yes a girl was singing
below and his lips parted too
I mean mine it was me

though I didn't know
the words didn't know her name
what would happen once I did

it was the first day of May
a train clattered by not
far away soldiers were coming.

acknowledgments

Thank you to the editors and readers of the journals in which many of these poems first appeared, often in earlier versions: 32 *Poems, Bennington Review, Cave Wall, Cherry Tree, Conduit, Consequence, Cortland Review, Dash, Field, Glacier, Inkwell Magazine, Memorious, New Limestone Review, On the Seawall, Poetry Northwest, Prairie Schooner, Thimble Literary Magazine, Tiferet,* and *Tupelo Quarterly.*

"Mother's Silver Teapot" was published by Broadsided Press as a digital broadside, with art by Meghan Keane, in 2020. "The Stag" also appeared in *The Best American Poetry 2020* (Scribner, 2020). An earlier version of "There's This String" was set to music by composer Matthew Henning and performed at the Firehouse Space Festival in Brooklyn in 2013. It was also reprinted in *Innisfree Poetry Journal.*

The first glimmers of inspiration for these poems came from reading Jean Follain, in translations by Christopher Middleton and Kurt Heinzelman. I'm grateful to Keith Taylor for all kinds of writerly advice, including tipping me off to the mystery and wonder in Follain's poems. I also wish to express my gratitude for the music of the great Scott Joplin, which has been in my ears since I first heard "The Entertainer" as a boy, and which helped me hear this world and imagine Uncle Albert. I listened to Joshua Rifkin's, Richard Zimmerman's, and Alexander Peskanov's recordings of Joplin's music repeatedly while working on this book.

Thank you to Ava Leavell Haymon and everyone at LSU Press for their generosity, careful attention, and continuing support of my work. Thank you to Aaron Caycedo-Kimura and Rhett Iseman Trull for their enthusiastic close readings of early versions of this book and their many insightful suggestions. I'm grateful to Leslie Harrison for the beautiful example of *The Book of Endings* and for sharing her thoughts on writing without punctuation, which helped me piece together David's fractured voice. Once again, I want to thank Stuart Greenhouse and Jay Leeming, my old friends in poetry.

And always my family: This book is for Dad, Mom, Lillian, and Preston.

notes

The epigraph is a quotation from Seamus Heaney's poem "Mint" from *The Spirit Level* (Farrar, Straus and Giroux, 1997).

"To Tighten and to Tune" is for Bob Thorburn.

"Wouldn't Hold" is for Barb Thorburn.

"There's This String" owes a debt to William Stafford's poem "The Way It Is" from *The Way It Is: New & Selected Poems* (Graywolf Press, 1999).

"The Fisherman" reimagines a scene from *The Tin Drum,* by Günter Grass.